0 024 663 94X 1F

KT-387-796

Renew online at https://catalogue.sefton.gov.uk/.

Or by telephone at any Sefton library:
Bootle: 0151 934 5781   Meadows: 0151 288 6727

Crosby: 0151 257 6400   Netherton: 0151 525 0607

Formby: 01704 874177   Southport: 0151 934 2118

A fine will be charged on any overdue item plus the cost of reminders sent

Paintball Panic

Robin and Chris Lawrie

Illustrated by
Robin Lawrie

Acknowledgements

The authors and publishers would like to thank Julia Francis, Hereford Diocesan Deaf Church lay co-chaplain, for her help with the sign language in the *Chain Gang* books, and Dr Cathy Turtle, ecologist, for her help with the selection of species in books 13 to 18.

Published by Evans Brothers Limited
2A Portman Mansions
Chiltern Street
London W1U 6NR

© Robin and Christine Lawrie
First published 2004

The authors assert their moral right to be identified as the authors of this work in accordance with the Copyright, Designs and Patents Act, 1988.

Printed in Hong Kong

British Library Cataloguing in Publication data.
Lawrie, Robin
  Paintball Panic. – (The Chain Gang)
  1. Slam Duncan (Fictitious character) – Juvenile fiction
  2. All terrain cycling – Juvenile fiction 3. Adventure stories
  4. Children's stories
  I. Title II. Lawrie, Chris
  823.9'14[J]

ISBN 0 237 525593

Hi, my name is 'Slam' Duncan.

I ride and race downhill mountain bikes with a group of friends. We call ourselves 'The Chain Gang'.

We train on a big hill called Westridge behind our village, Shabberley.
Sometimes there are races there, too.
For a long time everything was just great.
But recently there have been problems.

*I'm Andy. (Andy is deaf and signs instead of talking.)

5

Lots of new people have moved into our village. They all want to use our hill, too. But not for mountain biking.

We now have dog walkers using OUR trails!

Not to mention joggers . . .

horse riders . . .

and worst of all,
motor bikers . . .

ROAR ROAR VROOM

. . . who churn
our courses
into porridge.

11

That night I had a great idea.
I'd get up a petition
among all the new
village people who
used the hill. I'd tell them what was
happening. I'd get lots of signatures.
First I tried the dog walkers.

Not my problem, mate. I can walk the dog anywhere! Besides, my daughter needs a house in the village.

GRRRR!

Then the joggers.

No way, chum, I'm a builder and I could use some work. I can jog anywhere.

On the way home from school next day
we looked in the Tuer Cycles shop window.

It was all a bit of a surprise!

Later, on my paper round, I was talking to Miss Soames, the sheep farmer.

On the way home I caught up
with Fionn on the edge
of Westridge. She was
having problems
with Baggage.
Horses can be
startled by bikes
coming up quietly
behind them. I should have spoken earlier.

Well, Slam, that's just typical of your stupid behaviour. Dozy and I are pretty fed up with the whole paintball business. We all know where playing with guns ends up.

I could see her point. But Larry, Andy and
I had decided to give it a go. We couldn't
back out now. Besides, it looked like fun.

Saturday: the day of the Westridge Developments paintball tournament. The paintballers caused a huge jam in the lanes and managed to upset just about everyone including . . .

. . . Miss Soames and
her dog, a horse rider,
a couple of walkers and
Fionn's dad on his tractor.
A paintballer splatted a motorbiker's
leather jacket with a paintball. Good
thing the owner didn't see who did it!

Up at Westridge car park the organisers explained paintball rules.

Punk Tuer, our dodgy biking rival,
appeared with shiny new kit.

The game began. Everybody was splatting everybody. Andy, Larry and I laid low.

Then everybody argued about who was dead or not.

23

So it was game over for the Chain Gang.
But on the way back to the gun hire . . .

25

I went straight home, but Andy and Larry went the long way over the hills. That evening Andy texted me what happened.

Fionn had come roaring up to them.

You stupid little boys! Look what you've done. I've been trying to round up our sheep but now thanks to your silly guns I can't tell which are ours!
Didn't you know they were colour coded? Ours have pink splodges. Miss Soames' have yellow splodges. Harry Nockold's have blue splodges. Now they all look like walking rainbows.
Oops!

Andy and Larry made their escape!

But as I was reading
the text message . . .

YIPES!

. . . lots of angry people were turning up
outside – dog walkers, joggers, horse
riders and farmers.

C'Mon out, Slam. We want to talk to you.

I knew there was no point in hiding.
So I went to the door.

OK, Slam, where's that petition? We don't want this paint balling nonsense every weekend.

WESTRIDGE DEVELOPMENTS MUST GO!